MW01069959

Meet the Chaplain

Sharlotte Druex
Just Jesus Ministries

The Matthew 25 Project

"Then these righteous ones will reply, 'Lord, when did we ever see you hungry and feed you? Or thirsty, and gave you something to drink? Or a stranger, and showed you hospitality? Or naked, and gave you clothing? When did we ever see you sick or in prison and visit you?' "And the King will say, 'I tell you the truth, when you did it to one of the least of these people, you were doing it to me!'"

Matthew 25:35-40

Foreword

This book has been written as an instruction manual for those desiring to improve their knowledge and skill in reaching out to the unreachable.

As the Director of *Just Jesus Ministries*, Chaplain Druex has provided all the tools necessary to prepare the reader for encounters with people of all walks of life. No matter where in the world you go, this book will prove instrumental in assisting you in the Great Commission, of winning souls for the Kingdom of God.

Chaplain Druex's own testimony will also assist you in opening the minds of people you encounter, and prompt them to make a decision for Christ.

Thirty three years ago, I too was reaching out to people in the remote villages of India, with very few tools, and only my personal testimony to offer. As a result, many people accepted the Lord as their personal Savior. By His grace and mercy, the Lord prompted me to build churches in different parts of India, and the Middle Eastern countries. Today, we have five churches in the Middle East, and two in India; and still many more will be built for the expansion of His Kingdom. Likewise, this book will make you a Fisher of Men.

Pastor Nalinee D. Tillman

Lilly of the Valley Ministries

Foreword

I am the Director and founder of the Saints of Value World Ministerial Training Center, Norwalk, California.

What an honor it is to comment about this great and powerful woman of God, Chaplain Sharlotte Druex, founder of *Just Jesus Ministries*.

I have witnessed her faithfulness and obedience to God throughout the years. Chaplain Sharlotte has a tremendous heart for the less fortunate. I have witnessed her power and expertise this past decade, as she moves in the Holy Spirit over the homeless and incarcerated.

The manual she has written is awesome. The anointed guidelines are designed for ministers to easily use these principles, and will profoundly change their ministry effectiveness forever.

Dr. / Pastor Vicki M. Lee
Saints of Value World Ministries

About This Manual

By Elder D. R. Jones

This manual is a guide to making outreach ministry both simple and applicable. The simple principals contained herein have proved successful for *Just Jesus Ministries,* again and again. As we explore the various aspects of bringing salvation to the lost, this manual addresses the incarcerated, as well as the homeless. Statistics, relating to the incarcerated and homeless are astounding; therefore, you will agree that this manual is timely, and will assist churches and ministries to reach out to these affected individuals quickly and effectively; many of whom are children! This manual also gives counsel concerning preparation, procedures, and intercessory prayer. This manual also directs attention on how to analyze the individual's mental state, read their behavior, and getting to the root of their dysfunction. Although the principals herein are basic, they have been very fruitful, and begin with a heart-wrenching, transparent testimony of Chaplain Druex's personal journey into Christ.

Table of Contents

Chapter 1

The Chaplain's Personal Testimony

Prior to receiving the Lord Jesus Christ as Personal Savior, Chaplain Sharlotte Druex experienced the harsh realities of life on the street, and her introduction into the bizarre life of the underworld began as a young adult.

Sharlotte started working as a call girl at the age of 27, and later became a drug dealer. Before long, she ended up as a drug addict. With her head-long plunge into darkness now complete, she found herself involved in various, felonious crimes, such as bank fraud and grand-theft auto, just to name a few.

But God, in his mercy, preserved her life. Amazingly, Sharlotte never faced conviction for any of these crimes. Once arrested, she faced incarceration, but only for unpaid traffic tickets.

During her former life, Sharlotte experienced the extreme highs and the lows of the sinful lifestyle. Satan caused her to prosper in material and financial wealth, which was the perfect bait of deception for a young woman like her.

Like so many women trapped in that lifestyle, Satan pampered her as a lamb, and all the while prepared her for slaughter. She soon recognized how far from her moral foundation she had strayed. Sharlotte's parents instilled a good moral foundation in her, but it was not enough to shield her from childhood traumas that would shape her path in life for the next twenty years.

Storm clouds raged against Sharlotte early in life. Circumstances and conditions developed, which separated her from her family. For instance, she came to find out that she did not know her biological father, which caused her a great deal confusion. As a young child, she also suffered a three-year separation from her family, which resulted in many sorrows, including sexual molestation at the age five. Meantime, the scars of resentment grew deep in Sharlotte.

The instability during this time in her young life, resulted in the development of certain behavioral flaws, which were not evident prior to the separation from her family.

As a result, Sharlotte became a rebellious and defiant teenager who refused to submit to authority. Because of her defiance, Sharlotte's mother sought the aid of the juvenile authorities. Their diagnoses of Sharlotte indicated that she was "just a spoiled child in need of corporal punishment." It was advice that only fueled the conflict between Sharlotte and her parents.

The methods used to correct her included long-term confinements to her room at home. As the seasons passed, Sharlotte continued to be confined to her room, while trying to process the reasons for life's harsh realities, and her confinement did nothing to ease her rage, but only served to exacerbate her rebellious attitude. Unable to cope with the turbulence brewing in her home, she became a runaway.

As a runaway teenager, Sharlotte got pregnant, which presented yet another insurmountable challenge in her life. The pregnancy caused Sharlotte to incur toxicema, which is the presence of toxins in the blood. Sharlotte's life, and that of her unborn infant's, was now in danger, and both almost died. Who would live? The mother or her baby? A decision had to be made.

In the last remaining moments, with their lives being uncertain, a specialist discovered the possibility of saving them both. By the grace of God, both Sharlotte and her baby boy survived. While the hospital struggled to save her life on the delivery table, Sharlotte had a near-death experience.

She left her body and arrived at the gates of heaven. From behind the gates, a voice spoke, "That now is not your time." Coming back to consciousness, she soon recovered and her infant son was born healthy and whole. It was a joyous occasion for her, and the prospects of finally having a stable family life of her own, looked promising.

Sharlotte actually married soon after the baby arrived, and moved to Ohio. But a few years later, the raging storm fell upon her again, and came to destroy her momentary happiness.

Her young son was hit by a car at the age of three, which left him in a coma for several days. The doctors gave him little or no life expectancy, and said, "If he survives, he will be no more than a vegetable."

However, the day came when God once again revealed His mercy to Sharlotte. A mysterious woman came into the hospital to pray for another little girl, and happened upon the room where Sharlotte's son lay. And, she laid hands on him and prayed. The woman began to speak in an unknown language that Sharlotte had never heard. After praying for about an hour, the mysterious visitor departed.

Six hours later, the doctors called Sharlotte at home with exciting news. A miracle had occurred! Her son had awakened from his coma.

The residual effects of the accident were that he was like an infant. Because of the trauma, physical therapy was necessary, but within a year, he was restored to a normal, active four-year old boy.

Sharlotte again enjoyed a short season of happiness. Her little family moved to Texas where, within a few years, the marriage was plagued by alcohol and physical abuse. The storm clouds once again consumed her life.

On several occasions, Sharlotte took her son and fled for her life, due to her husband's drunken assaults. After trying to reconcile the marriage, things only got worse. After being assaulted and threatened by her husband with a gun, she made the decision to leave once and for all, and get a divorce.

Sharlotte had been a Wal-Mart warehouse supervisor for eight years, and once her divorce was final, returned to California with her son, and took an early retirement.

It was now the year 1988, and the stress of being the single parent of a growing teenage son, once again set Sharlotte on a familiar path of need and destitution. She entered the call-girl business. (Thankfully, Sharlotte never had more than three clients.) And, striving for additional financial stability, she also became a drug dealer to maximize her profits from both endeavors.

Things looked quite profitable with the emergence of a new designer drug, known as Crystal Meth; but it plunged Sharlotte into an even deeper darkness than before.

Soon after her introduction to Crystal Meth, she became addicted and the doors of opportunity, as well the profits she earned, dwindled away. Now bereft of the high times and new-found prosperity, the grief and sorrow of sin took hold of Sharlotte's life as never before.

Before long, all the horrors of the addiction entrapped her, with no way out. She was now a universe away from the morals she once embraced in her family's home. The utter death-grip of this addiction drove her to places that she would ordinarily have never dared enter.

At this point in time, only God could bring deliverance from her suffering and grief. Sharlotte's friend saw her predicament, and suggested God as her way out. The friend introduced Sharlotte to prayer, and during this period, demonic forces began to manifest around Sharlotte, such as the hands of a clock moving counter-clockwise and inanimate objects such as dolls, coming to life.

While at a drug-house in November of 1993, God spoke to Sharlotte and told her to go home. She got up and left immediately. Upon arriving at home, the Lord gave her a vision, warning her that if she continued on the path she was travelling, her death was certain. In the vision, she also saw three separate personal disasters that the enemy planned for her, which eventually came true, but the Lord rescued her from all of them.

This experience led Sharlotte to see the need for change in her life. The problem was, she just didn't know how to implement the change. Sharlotte was untrained in prayer, and yet she began to seek God. Her prayer time started small and grew into hours of prayer. In the agony of her spirit she cried out," God if you are real, save me from this life, or I will die."

Sharlotte also expressed a desire to actually see the works of God. She prayed, "God, I do not want to be one of those old ladies that pray and never get answers." This went on for months, during which time the events in the vision happened.

Because God warned Sharlotte through the vision, she escaped the tragic events.

One year later, in November of 1994, while wrestling to overcome her addiction, Sharlotte reached her lowest point.

All her friends were nowhere in sight, she had no money or food left, and her rent was due. It was during this low point that God delivered her. He saved her, set her free, and filled her with His Holy Spirit.

She was soon free from drugs and the dark life was behind her. Immediately, God began to move in supernatural ways for her. Over the next few days, He showed her His provision by supplying her with the food, and the money she needed for rent.

In November, 1995, Sharlotte faced another devastating storm, when she lost her mother to cancer; but this time, she felt the hand of the Lord holding her steady, unlike all those other times.

Soon after her salvation, Sharlotte began attending services at *Lily of the Valley Ministries.* This became her home church, under the leadership of Pastor Nalinee D. Tillman, who became a spiritual mother to Sharlotte.

Eventually, Sharlotte began attending *The City of God Church*, under the leadership of Pastor K. S. Bailey, where she received vital teaching that helped her to grow substantially. Sharlotte founded the *Bind and Touch Project*, whose mission was to collect and donate toys for less fortunate children. God spoke to her during this time, and made her conscious of the call He placed on her life. However, the devil was not finished vying for her life just yet.

After she came into the knowledge of her call to ministry, Satan urged her to leap from the window of a two-story building. This was designed, of course, to stop her from fulfilling the call of God.

In June of 1999, Sharlotte attended *Saints of Value Ministries in Norwalk, California*, and was officially ordained as a Minister of Christ. While there, she served as treasurer for a season, and eventually became an instructor, at *Saints of Value Ministerial Training Center.*

After being ordained, Satan appeared to her in the form of a hideous imp. It was yet another attempt to frighten her from the call and work set before her. However, through the Spirit of God, she overcame this visitation.

Today, Chaplain Sharlotte Druex, is the founder and director of *Just Jesus Ministries,* an organization that feeds and provides the personal needs of the homeless around the Orange County area.

In April of 2010, she felt the Lord leading her back to school, whereupon she was ordained as a Chaplain of jails and prisons.

She serves as a Chaplain at the Orange County women's Jail, where she ministers to the incarcerated. Sharlotte is also a fervent intercessor. God has opened new doors for Chaplain Druex, wherein she is able to target the hurting through seminars, conferences and many other ministries.

Among her recognitions, Chaplain Druex has served on the Mayor's Prayer Breakfast Committee, has received Community Recognition and Certification by the Orange County Rescue Mission, and the State Senate Office of California.

Chaplain Druex has received many invitations to be guest speaker at various prisons and correctional facilities, and made numerous guest appearances on various Christian talk shows.

Chaplain Druex has given this testimony to encourage others that God is faithful, and will help all that call on him.

Remember, we overcome by the Blood of the Lamb, and the word of our testimony (Revelations 12:11); hence the reason for this manual. When you see a homeless or incarcerated person, you will never know what traumas they experienced, to put them there. They were all once children. Bad people don't just grow on trees. The unseen predator's one and only mission is to destroy lives. But Christ gave us the power to rescue them.

God Bless you,

Chaplain Sharlotte Druex

Welcome To

Just Jesus Ministries

Ezekiel 36:25-29

1.   The call to salvation
2.   The call to discipleship
3.   Commitment to the Great Commission

Chapter 2

Getting Organized

Tattered clothes, body odor, messy hair, intoxicated, depressed, or maybe just jobless; unfortunately, this is a reality for so many people today. It's a trap set by the enemy to destroy mankind.

Society says: They're lazy druggies and worthless.

Politicians say: Sweep them under the carpet.

The Feds say: We can't fit them into the budget.

Statistics show: Every family has at least one family member that is either homeless, using drugs, mentally unstable, or jobless.

Reality says: The majority of the population is at least one or two paychecks away from being homeless.

But Jesus said:

> "Then these righteous ones will reply, 'Lord,
> when did we ever see you hungry and feed
> you? Or thirsty, and gave you something to
> drink? Or a stranger, and showed you hospi-
> tality? Or naked, and gave you clothing?
> When did we ever see you sick or in prison
> and visit you?' And the King will say, 'I tell
> you the truth, when you did it to one of the
> least of these people, you were doing it to
> me!'"
>
> Matthew 25:35-40

Homeless Statistics

In one city survey, 94% of people were homeless. The study also showed that in the United States, there are 100% more homeless people, than there are homeless shelters, in any given city. The National Law Center on Homelessness also rendered the following findings:

> ➤ 70% of all homeless have no shelter at all
> ➤ 64% are mentally challenged and/or drug addicted
> ➤ 60% live in cars

- 25% live in cardboard tents
- 76% of all homeless persons are single males
- 30% of all homeless persons are single females
- 30% of the homeless are families with children

As the church, we must all do our part to relieve this situation. If we cannot get out doing hands-on outreach, we can at least pray for these lives to change, and/or donate financial assistance for programs addressing these needs.

Now, concerning the incarcerated, the 2009 U.S. Inmate Statistics issued by the Federal Department of Justice shows that 2,279,400 inmates were incarcerated in adult prisons, while an additional 93,000 youth spent detention in Juvenile Halls.

Being homeless has become a nationwide epidemic here in America. Now that your ministry has answered the call that the Lord placed upon you, you should get ready to be sent out. Take a look:

> Then I heard the voice of the Lord, saying,
> "Whom shall I send, and who will go for
> us?" And I answered, "Here I am; send me."

Be a very committed team. Believe that God has commissioned you to labor in this particular vineyard, to be a light in a very dark place. Be committed to taking back what the enemy has stolen. Believe that the answer to change is feeding and clothing those in need. Believe that, if a person recognizes the one and only Savior, Jesus Christ, and submits to his authority in their lives, things will change in supernatural ways.

Salvation should be your number one focus, and by meeting the needs of the destitute, allows the Holy Spirit to move in their lives. And then, we can minister to their spiritual needs.

The Order of Business

Choosing a Team

The first order of business is to pray to the Lord to send you a dedicated team. The Lord will show you whom to choose. Concerning qualifications, team members must:

➢ Be saved and sanctified

➢ Confess that Jesus Christ is Lord, that He was born of a virgin, died on the cross for our sins, and rose from the dead on the third day

➢ Be spirit-filled with the baptism of the Holy Spirit, with the evidence of speaking in other tongues

➢ Confess the scriptures of the Holy Bible as the Word of God

➢ Display an outward and earnest interest in the work of the jail and homeless ministries.

Schedule A Team Meeting

The second order of business is to schedule a meeting with your team and determine your policies and operations. Upon conclusion of your meeting, your team should:

➢ Determine whether the team is spiritually prepared to participate in the homeless or jail outreach.

➢ Discuss how to initiate outreach to the homeless or incarcerated person.

➢ Discuss how to lead the homeless and inmate to salvation.

➢ Have ready the necessary supplies to document the new soul; eg: a log listing saved souls (optional).

➢ Discuss how to relate to them right where they are, spiritually.

➢ Discuss team member conduct. For instance: how to know when things get too personal between the team member and the inmate/homeless person, etc.

Schedule weekly meetings, or as many as possible, to keep the vision and work on track, in a unified and organized manner.

Preparation

Preparation for this ministry must be covered with much prayer. Make sure that you cover the preparatory aspects of the ministry, not only prior to an outreach service, but also throughout the year.

Allow the Holy Spirit to lead you as you place the right person in each area of ministry, for each outreach service.

As you pray, the Spirit of God will go before you and soften the hearts of your guests.

Throughout the year, prepare for each service, making sure you have all necessary food, clothing items, hygiene products, Bible tracts, Bibles, and teaching handouts.

The primary goal for the
homeless & jail ministries is:

SALVATION!

Of the millions of active believers world-wide, only a small number are actually involved in ministry to the homeless, despite the fact that we see these displaced persons on almost every street corner, in most recreational parks, and pretty much all over the downtown area. No community has been unaffected. When seeing these people on the street, we feel that giving them a quarter, a piece of bread, or even springing for a McDonald's meal, we have done our duty; but is this really enough? Some people do engage in feeding and clothing the destitute on a regular basis, and it's all right to meet their physical needs; **but if we neglect the spiritual needs of that person, we have been of no service to them.** The scriptural mandates are perfectly clear. Bringing them **salvation** is our first priority!

The Many Functions of This Ministry

Every believer should be involved in a homeless ministry to some capacity. There are many ways to be involved:

> - Provide prayer support
> - Volunteer your time with a ministry
> - Donate food and/or clothing
> - Donate special offerings

We cannot encourage you enough to understand, that the most essential way to assist in this area, is to:

PRAY PRAY PRAY PRAY PRAY

Chapter 3

Understanding Intercession

Intercession builds a road from the gates of hell, to the gates of heaven in the spiritual realm. In fact, every time we intercede, the road is being constructed for the lost soul to walk upon, away from hell and up to the Kingdom.

1st Timothy 2:1
I urge you, first of all, to pray for all people. Ask God to help them; intercede on their behalf, and give thanks for them.

The more we intercede, the more foundations are being laid. Each time we stop intercession, 'construction' of the road's foundation ceases; but continued intercession makes us co-workers with Christ.

Jesus interceded for hours. As a result, his miracles manifested immediately. When we intercede, it collapses space and time, until there is only the throne of God before us. Through intercession, we are able to go boldly to the throne of grace on behalf of others, and submit requests concerning their needs. In turn, the Lord gives us the needed supplies, to pass them on to the destitute. Intercession is designed by God to attack an earthly problem in the spirit realm. The way it works is very simple:

> A problem comes along ... the intercessor brings it
> to the attention of the Lord ... and He dispatches
> the supplies and/or answer.

Jesus said in Matthew 7:7, "Ask and you shall receive." He is faithful and will provide you with everything you need for this ministry; after all, it's His ministry. It is through the warring prayers of intercessors that the strongholds of Satan are torn down. In this way, millions of souls are ushered into the Kingdom of God, and lives will be changed. As you prepare to enter this ministry, you place yourself in a position to fight the battle.

Ephesians 6:18
Pray in the Spirit at all times and on every occasion. Stay alert and be persistent in your prayers for all believers everywhere.

Items to Intercede About

Seek God for his instructions, in the same way that the early Christians did, leading up to the Day of Pentecost, as outlined in Acts 1:24-25. When conducting an outreach service, always remember that the SOUL is the most important thing. The Lord said, "He that wins souls is wise." Therefore, organize a service exclusively to win souls. Start intercession with everyone on your team and **make it mandatory** for them to be involved. Then intercede concerning the following:

1. Pray for SOULS to be saved

2. Seek God for people who have the gift of COMPASSION

3. Pray for the souls' deliverance, restoration, stability and shelter (things that lost people need)

4. Pray for God to meet every need they have

5. Pray for God to lead them to a church; not just any church, but a Bible-teaching, spirit-filled church; because the anointing destroys the yoke.

Once God establishes the team, assign each team member to a specific task in the service. For instance, assign someone to intercede during the service; another to lead praise and worship; another to deliver the word and minister the altar call; and yet another to minister to those came forward for salvation. Keep an accurate count of new souls and rededications, for your own records and encouragement.

If you are conducting a service at a location where souls can come and go freely, the order of the service should proceed as follows.

1. Feed the spirit first, by conducting the service

2. Give them food second

3. Then, hand out clothing, hygienic supplies, blankets, etc

If you are conducting a service where souls are confined to the building, the order of the service can be more flexible:

1. Give them food first

2. Feed the spirit second, by conducting the service

3. Then hand out clothing, hygienic supplies, blankets, etc

The Intercessory Prayer Checklist

Intercessory prayer is called for by God to address the following:

- Make ready the homeless and incarcerated to receive salvation
- Bring in donations for the outreach
- The welfare of the homeless and incarcerated
- Upcoming events in your outreach or ministry
- All outreaches, churches, ministries and all spiritual leaders
- Other ministries associated with your outreach
- For God to raise up someone in the White House with compassion for the homeless
- For God to open shelters
- For your personal families and their lives
- In addition, whatever God lays on your hearts

Intercessory is mandatory for all:

- Leaders
- Staff
- Volunteers

Chapter 4

Going Into

The Enemy's Camp

The enemy's camp is a place dominated by ... well ... the enemy! As such, it is saturated with sin, sinful behaviors, blindness to sins, and every propensity toward sin imaginable. And make no mistake; the enemy does not want you there.

God called the enemy's camp a place of great darkness, absent of any kind of light. People who live in darkness have lost their ability to "reason" and know the difference between right and wrong. For this reason, when the Lord hung on the cross for hours on end, he said, "Father, forgive them. They don't know what they are doing."

This is true of people living in total darkness. And the symptoms of sin are many: drug addiction, homelessness, imprisonment, prostitution, child abuse, starvation, disease, lack of medical attention, utter despair, and the utter waste of humanity.

So what are we actually talking about, here? Some third-world country? No ... just downtown Orange County. Or, go to any inner-city skid row area, and you will see the full impact of generational, human waste, as a result of the enemy's work.

Thank God Jesus is the light of the world. He is the lamp unto their path, and their bright light in the middle of midnight.

It stirs up the devil when the saints come stomping into his camp and steal back what he has stolen. The souls of lost men and women are Satan's most prized possession, because he knows their destruction is the only thing that pierces God, right through His heart.

Ezekiel 18:4
Behold, all souls are Mine; the soul of the father as
well as the soul of the son is Mine. The soul that
sins shall die.

While we are in the enemy's camp, we need to make sure that we are prayed up and built up in our most holy faith. In other words, put yourself in the presence of the Lord the entire time you are in there.

In order for God to manifest Himself in us, and take back what the enemy has stolen, we must be **qualified saints** for God to work in us, and through us. We must be Spirit-filled hearers and doers of the word; not just on the day that we enter the enemy's camp, but in our daily walk with the Lord. In fact, the holier our walk, the greater His manifestation through us on the day we enter the enemy's camp.

Act 1:8

But you will receive power when the Holy Spirit comes upon you. And you will be my witnesses, telling people about me everywhere, in Jerusalem, throughout Judea, Samaria, and to the ends of the earth.

Know also what your weapons are, and how to apply them effectively when confronting the enemy. Know that you are more than a conqueror through Christ Jesus, and when entering the enemy's camp, walk in that power and authority.

As such, the enemy sees the Blood of Jesus and trembles and flees in seven different directions, which is exactly the effect you are going for. It is of the utmost importance to follow **God's instructions** by putting on the whole armor of God for battle:

Ephesians 6:10-18

A final word: Be strong in the Lord and in his mighty power. Put on all of God's armor so that you will be able to stand firm against all strategies of the devil. For we are not fighting against flesh-and-blood enemies, but against evil rulers and authorities of the unseen world, against mighty powers in this dark world, and against evil spirits in the heavenly places. Therefore, put on every piece of God's armor so you will be able to resist the enemy in the time of evil. Then after the battle you will still be standing firm. Stand your ground, putting on the belt of truth and the body armor of God's righteousness. For shoes, put on the peace that comes from the Good News so that you will be fully prepared. In addition to all of these, hold up the shield of faith to stop the fiery arrows of the devil. Put on salvation as your helmet, and take the sword of the Spirit, which is the word of God. Pray in the Spirit at all times and on every occasion. Stay alert and be persistent in your prayers for all believers everywhere.

The lost are under the control of demonic spirits (Ephesians 2:2; Colossians 1:13-14). Most are unaware that disobedience to God allows the enemy to work in and through their lives. Jesus is the light that shines and dispels ignorance (1ˢᵗ John 2:8).

The saint is filled with the Spirit of God and equipped to battle for the souls of the lost Satan has held men and women captive, but one stronger than Satan lives in the saints. (Matthew 12:28-29). Below, God continues to give cautious wisdom into spiritual warfare.

2ⁿᵈ Corinthians 10:3-6

We are human, but we don't wage war as humans do. We use God's mighty weapons, not worldly weapons, to knock down the strongholds of human reasoning and to destroy false arguments. We destroy every proud obstacle that keeps people from knowing God. We capture their rebellious thoughts and teach them to obey Christ. And after you have become fully obedient, we will punish everyone who remains disobedient.

1. We need to be sure the people we take into the enemy's camp are living a holy life

2. Out of necessity, they must be prayer warriors and intercessors

3. Have a working knowledge of spiritual warfare and how to fight through the spirit of God

4. Understand the importance of putting on the whole armor of God to be able to withstand the enemy's attacks

5. Be sure they understand God's word and live by it

6. Leave no doors or areas in their lives open for attack, which means the practice of sin

Chapter 5

Understanding The Personal Relationship With Jesus

In the book of Matthew 13:18, Jesus taught us about the parable of the sower, and the seed. As His representatives, we need to be sure that the word we teach is solid, and based upon actual scriptures.

With careful preparation of the heart, the seed of God's word will fall on good ground. This is accomplished by breaking up the fallow (hardened) ground, and thorns and weeds of the heart (Hosea 10:12). Then, after the fallow ground is softened, we can plant the word of God, making sure that the word has been correctly dissected.

We are to teach the new disciple the importance of having a solid foundation, and filling them with the desire for the sincere milk of the word. We should teach them that salvation is a matter of the heart, and that all relationships need intimacy with God. Below, is a list of scriptures pertaining to salvation, to share with the new disciple:

> John 3:16
> Romans 10: 9-10
> 1st Peter 1:18-19
> Ephesians 2:8
> Titus 2:11-14

Once they have received the Lord as Savior, teach them the following skills, to assist them in their walk in this New Life:

> Praying to get results: Matthew 7:7-8

> Warn them that the devil will attempt to reclaim them, because he usually returns to a 'clean house': Matthew 12:43-45

> How to resist the devil and put on the armor of God: James 4:7 and Ephesians 6:10-14

> Seeking first the Kingdom of God for everything, after which all other things will be granted: Matthew 6:33

➤ That their relationship will require daily communication with the Lord, through prayer, and reading of His word: John 15:7

After the new disciple understands the dynamics of his/her relationship with God, outline what the Lord will do for them.

God's Promises

Tell the new disciple that they now have access to a TREASURE TROVE of promises available to them, everything from healing of the mind and body, to wealth and success in all they do. Tell them also that they now have angels assigned to them, to watch over them every moment they are awake or asleep.

Psalms 91 (excerpts)

He that stays under the wings of God Almighty will find rest and protection. For the Lord will rescue you from every deadly trap. He will cover you with his feathers and shelter you under His wings. His faithful promises are your armor and protection. Do not be afraid of the terrors of the night, nor of the disaster that strikes in broad daylight. Though ten thousand are dying all around you, the evil will never touch you, because the angel of the Lord has surrounded you, in case you so much as stub your toe!

Galatians 3:13-14

For Christ was struck with the curse, so that you would be rescued from the curse. Furthermore, you have received the blessings of Abraham.

You should inform the new disciple that "the curse" spoken of above is ... poverty, disease, and never-ending destruction. Then inform him/her, that "the blessings of Abraham" are health, prosperity and success in all they do! Furthermore, the scripture passage below highlights the extent of God's cleansing of their entire lives and souls:

Ezekiel 36:25-29

Then I will sprinkle clean water on you, and you will be clean. Your filth will be washed away, and you will no longer worship idols. And I will give you a new heart, and put a new spirit in you. I will take out your stony, stubborn heart and give you a tender, responsive heart, and put my Spirit in you, so that you will follow my decrees and be careful to obey my regulations. And you will live in the Promised Land. You will be My people, and I will be your God. I will give you prosperity, and stop every famine from attacking you.

Chapter 6

Understanding
The Sin Nature

In your encounters with inmates and especially the homeless, we need to explore the root of the problem in each individual, case by case; in other words, address the destruction that put them into that position in the first place.

Other than their sin nature, what else is going on with that individual? How did this problem get so deeply rooted inside of them? (Psalms. 51:5) If we look at the mind of a serial killer, we will find that 99.99% of the time, some extreme trauma happened to them during their childhood. In fact, when it happened, they felt so utterly helpless, the only way for them to relieve the reoccurring anguish, is to kill. More likely than not, it is impossible to rehabilitate them, but for Christ; hence, they need to be locked up.

Take for instance, Charles Manson. His mother was a prostitute and clinical schizophrenic back in the 1930s. She would often take Charlie, then just a tiny, thin, five-year old boy, and make him join in her sexual activities with customers. Then, for no reason at all, she locked him in a 4' x 5' tool shed out in the backyard, for hours on end, barely clothed in the freezing, cold Ozark winter. What emerged from the tool shed was a mentally and spiritually dysfunctional individual.

Science has also proved that when a person is sexually abused as a child, their brain literally stops functioning properly. Whatever their particular mental dysfunction may be, it is the root of their repeat sin nature, also known as 'iniquity.'

Christ Jesus came to set the captive free and they can be delivered of any repetitive sin nature, and achieve victory in their lives, through Him, and He will do it surgically and supernaturally. The Apostle Paul told us how to understand the sin nature and how we can overcome it.

Romans 5:12 & 19

When Adam sinned, sin entered the world. Adam's sin brought death, so death spread to everyone, for everyone sinned. Because one person disobeyed God, many became sinners. In the same way, one other Person obeyed God, and as a result, many will be made righteous.

The sin nature manifests itself by displaying deeply rooted problems such as drugs, alcohol, sex, murder, and violence.

These are just some of the results of the sin nature separating mankind from God (Galatians 5:19-21). As much as the correctional system, judges, and doctors try to rehabilitate these individuals, 90 % of them are repeat offenders.

However, we as believers know that Jesus is the only answer, but if we fail to fulfill the Great Commission, as mandated in Matthew 28:18-20, these souls will continue to be lost and dysfunctional...and will die that way.

It is our duty to be used by God and minister the Words of Life to them. Hence, the remedy for the sin nature is JESUS. And as we prepare to go out, we should follow the Lord's instructions, which were to fast and pray, and believe God for their salvation.

We often get upset when we see the Nation of Islam, Catholic's and other services, win over people in jail and on the streets. If we, as God's fellow laborers, will come out of the churches and engage in more outreach where the harvest is actually ready, we could win countless souls for Christ.

And when a gang member, a potential serial killer, or a suicidal person, comes to our churches, we are all too often focused on their choice of scanty clothing, worldly behaviors and, perhaps bad language. But these things should never be of any concern to us because they came to church for help, and we should, therefore, give it to them. More often that not, these persons looking for help are ignored by the church, and leave, perhaps never to return again. The Lord is not pleased with this kind of negligent behavior.

After reading the prior passage of scripture addressed to us, the 'shepherds,' we can see that more serious warnings were ever written in the word. Indeed, we have a serious job to do. Here, God said that if we fail to reach out to the lost, He considers it be our fault.

We need to first concentrate on bringing them in, and after that, the Holy Spirit will transform their lives (2nd Corinthians 3:18). Our job is only to teach them with the love of Jesus, doing all things with compassion, and making sure they are never driven away from the church.

On the next page is a passage of scripture that gives us an indication as to the Lord's displeasure when we, as ministers, fail to attend properly to the flock given to our charge.

Chapter 6

Ezekiel 34:4-10

You have not taken care of the weak, nor tended the sick or bound up the injured. You have not gone looking for those who wandered away and are lost. Instead, you ruled them with harshness and cruelty. So my sheep have been scattered without a shepherd, and they are easy prey for any wild animal. They have wandered through all the mountains and all the hills, across the face of the earth, yet no one has gone to search for them. Therefore, you shepherds, hear the word of the Lord. As surely as I live, you abandoned My flock and left them to be attacked by every wild animal. And though you were My shepherds, you didn't search for them, when they were lost. You took care of yourselves and left the sheep to starve. Therefore, you shepherds, hear the word of the Lord: I now consider you to be My enemies, and will hold you responsible for what has happened to My flock. I will take away your right to feed My flock, and will stop you from feeding yourselves. I will rescue My flock from your mouths, and My sheep will no longer be your prey.

Dealing With Backsliders

While ministering to various types of backsliders, it is again crucial to get to the root of the problem. Properly exploring the reasons for their defection from the Lord will better equip you to heal that situation, and bring them back to the Lord.

You might start by telling them that, whatever happened while they were still in the church, the Lord had nothing to do with the offense. Don't forget, many people were taught that, "Nothing bad can happen, unless God allows it."

Other times, they believe that God actually "sent" the traumatic event to teach them something spiritual. In such cases, let them know that Satan comes only to steal, kill and destroy, and that Jesus comes only to give abundant life (John 10:10).

Read to them also James 1:16-17, which states, "Be not deceived beloved; every good and perfect gift comes from the Father of Lights, in whom there is no variation or change." These two scriptures alone should prove to them that the Lord was not involved in the trauma.

Once we establish the person's root cause of the sin nature, mental dysfunctions, and state of mind, we can correctly minister and pray for them. We cannot make shallow assumptions as to why they left the church or Jesus. On the other hand, many people left the church for frivolous reasons. Leaving God should never be an option; therefore, the minister should strive to bring them back.

James 5:19-20
My dear brothers and sisters, if someone among you wanders away from the truth and is brought back, you can be sure that whoever brings the sinner back will save that person from death and bring about the forgiveness of many sins.

Upon examining the individual, on a case by case basis, many reasons for their defection will emerge. The most frequent ones are:

1. They left the church for no apparent reason

2. The pastor or someone at the church drove them away

3. They felt the church failed them, somehow

4. They observed the pastor living a sin-filled life, and failed to obey the word he was preaching

5. They became overwhelmed by the responsibilities of life, and procrastinated their return to the church

6.   They harbor a difference of opinion, concerning the word
       of God.

7.   They are upset because God did not move when they felt
       He should have, and lost their confidence in Him.

As discussed earlier, we as ministry leaders need to ask questions and determine where the root of the problem lies. If you are unable to ask questions, intercede on the matter and gain wisdom from God.

In the Book of Jeremiah 2:13-14, God spoke to Jeremiah and said, "For my people have done two evil things: they have abandoned me, their fountain of living water...Why have they become slaves? Why have they been carried away as plunder?"

God instructed Jeremiah to tell the people to acknowledge their sins and repent. As leaders, it is our duty to help them recognize the root of their problems. After exploring the reasons, lead them back to Jesus, by applying the Gospels.

For instance, let's say that you are counseling a woman who attends church, but also lives with a man out of wedlock. You could start the conversation by reminding her that being married to God and "shacking up with the devil" can result in a divorce from God, so on and so forth. Below are additional scriptures that will assist you in your conversations with backslidden individuals:

➤ Luke 15:8-10   The lost coin
➤ Luke 15:11-32   The lost Son
➤ Matthew 12:43-45 The unclean spirit
➤ Matthew 28:20   Keeping the commandments
➤ Jeremiah 3:14   God's plea for them to return home
➤ Jeremiah 31:32   God offers a new covenant

Chapter 7

The

Jail & Prison

Ministry

Some inmates only come to a prison church service in order to get out of their cell? Is this true? Or, could it be a divine appointment set by God to set the captive free.

Jesus came that the inmates would have life, and have it more abundantly. We plant the seed, which is the word of God, into their hearts, and perhaps another ministry comes along to water that seed with more in-depth understanding.

For instance, let's say you tell an inmate about the protection God can give him, but this may not mean anything to him on Monday. However, then he gets beat up by other inmates on Friday. Suddenly, God's offer of protection speaks volumes to him. Just then, another ministry comes in, and he asks to speak with them to learn more about God's protection.

It's called planting and watering. God is the one who causes the seed to grow, and converts that new creature into Christ's image. Jailhouse ministry is simple when we apply intercessory prayer. The Holy Spirit is the one who draws in the soul of the individual, and no one can come to God unless the Spirit of God draws him or her. Encourage the inmate to trade their inmate number for their name written in the Lamb's book of life. Tell them:

Jesus knocks at the door of our hearts
Jesus is this way, the truth, and the light

Why does a person become a repeat offender? It is because society fails to get to the root of the problem, and sends them back to jail when they reoffend. This method is not the answer or the cure. Jesus is the answer!

He is also the Root Puller!

Jesus said that some evil spirits will not leave a person without prayer and fasting. Allow God to show you when this should be done, and over what inmate. If the inmate cannot remember or articulate where the root problem began, allow God also to show this to you, and why it began. This will require you to walk in the Spirit and under His anointing. Jail ministry can be simple and rewarding when led supernaturally of this Holy Spirit.

Time To Apply What We Learned

Once you feel that your team is ready to enter the jail/prison ministry, contact the Executive Chaplain at the local jail and/or prison, and ask for an application. They will ask you to furnish additional documentation also, therefore, be prepared to give them whatever they need to get you qualified. After your team has been approved, ask the Executive Chaplain to add your team to the roster to conduct services. And now, let's review the typical profile of a jail/prison service.

Order of Jail/Prison Service

1. The song leader leads the inmates in praise songs

2. The ministers each give testimonies, on where God brought them from

3. Other inmates may want to give their own testimony also

4. The word of the Lord is now delivered by the minister, outlining the following benefits of receiving Christ, such as: healing, prosperity, protection, and a new start in life

5. The alter call is now placed with the invitation to receive Christ as Savior, and/or for rededication.

6. Let the inmates give a show of hands to make the public confession unto salvation, according to Romans 10:9-10

Some ministries prefer to deliver the 'corporate prayer' of salvation, wherein everyone prays to receive Christ together. However, corporate prayer does not allow the individual to make their own decision.

Before the service begins, pray in the Spirit. Then, as the inmates come in, scan your eyes across the inmates. Choose two or three, as the Lord leads, and assign yourself to their souls. Intercede for them throughout the service.

During the call to salvation, encourage them to answer the call. Please be advised that the order of service is subject to change, depending on the facility.

Hebrews 13:3

Remember those in prison as though chained to them. Remember also those being mistreated, as if you felt their pain in your own bodies.

Communicate Effectively!

Be sure your audience understands what is being proclaimed. A simple salvation message that is sound and based on the word of God will suffice. Use a Bible and a spoken language that is easy for them to understand, such as the:

➤ New Living Translation

➤ American Standard

➤ Amplified Bible

➤ New King James

Chapter 8

The
Homeless Ministry

The Apostles said that it is not enough to say to a hungry or naked person, "Well, God bless you," and do nothing to help them. So, let's discuss the practical aspects of this ministry.

1st John 3:17 and James 2:15-17

But, if a Christian has money enough to live well, and sees a brother in need, and won't help him, how can the love of God be in him? Or, if you know someone who is in need of food and clothing, and you say to him, "Well, good-bye, God bless you. Stay warm and eat hearty!" and does not give him clothing or food, what good does that do? It isn't enough just to have faith. You must also do good works to prove that you have it. Faith that doesn't show good works is dead and useless!

Rounding Up Food & Clothing

To obtain supplies, such as Bibles and tracts, you can call the Bible Society. Look on the internet for the closest chapter near you. Your 501(c)(3) allows you to receive special discounts when buying in bulk from any Christian bookstore.

Or, if you have talented people on your team, you can save money by writing, drawing and creating your own tracts. Bible tracts do not have to come in the usual 2" x 3" booklet format. They can also be letter size sheets folded in half, or as a tri-fold brochure. To print each sheet front and back costs only 12 cents at your local copy shop.

Things That The Homeless Need

Homeless people need basic things, such as personal hygiene supplies in the form of soap, tooth paste, toothbrushes, combs, and bulkier items, such as blankets, winter coats and jackets. If families are involved, their children will need shoes and warm clothing also.

Your ministry can purchase these basic items with moneys received from donations, or you can send out letters to local churches in your area, asking for donations from their assemblies. Many times, going to see the pastors in person brings quicker and better results.

Before going to see the pastors, investigate the prices of the items you will be asking for. Check to see if certain suppliers offer discounts to 501(c)(3) ministries, if you buy in bulk. Research the most economical stores and pass the information along to the pastors to assist them in getting the most for their dollar. You could also offer to split the costs with them.

When speaking with the pastors, have your information and costs ready, or if sending by letter, type them out in an easy to read letter. For example, tell him, "I need a donation of one hundred tooth brushes and toothpaste." Give him the cost, the best store to get them at, and the date by which you need them.

You could also ask each individual church to donate one item each, such as...Church A for food...Church B for winter coats...and Church C for toys...so on and so forth. Choose churches that have the compassion of Christ.

Entering the Facility

The facility could be a city mission, shelter, or any other place where the homeless are being taken care of in your locality. Once you have gathered all your supplies for the homeless, round up the quantity you will need for the next facility. Make contact with the person in charge of the facility to verify the date and time available for your team to enter.

Make sure all the paperwork, if applicable, is fully approved before proceeding. Determine also how many supplies (food and clothing) you will need to bring with you:

> How many people will be attending?
> How many are men, and how many are women?
> Will children be attending?

Find out their preferred order of service, or prepare your own. Once in the facility, set up your tables and arrange the order of the service according to the facility's instructions.

Communicate Effectively

Be sure your audience understands what is being proclaimed. A simple salvation message that is sound and based on the word of God will suffice. Use a Bible and spoken language that is easy for them to understand, such as:

> New Living Translation
> American Standard
> Amplified Bible
> New King James

Remember to teach a simple salvation message, leading them to Jesus. When the invitation time comes, keep count of the souls that receive Jesus, for your records.

Designate Team Member Functions

What is the function and role of each team member? Establish them early so that there will be no confusion once in the facility. Following, is a list of the team member functions you may need for a smooth-running operation, once at the facility:

Hospitality Greeters

This team member is the first representative from your ministry to show the love of Christ to arriving guests, and must present a Christ-like manner. This team member makes sure all guests are given Bibles and other ministry hand-outs. They are also responsible to show guests to the clothing table in an orderly fashion.

Clothing Table Ministry

This team member assists the guests with love and patience as they choose clothing items, making sure that the line flows smoothly and in a timely manner.

Hygiene Table Ministry

As the guests are flowing to the hygiene table, this team member has to be courteous, loving, and very understanding to the needs of the guest. If the guest asks for a certain item that is not in the bags, inform them that upon our next visit we will make every effort to have that specific item available. The team member makes note of this with pen and paper.

Food Ministry

As the guests are eating their meal, this is a good opportunity, not only to break bread with them, but also to minister to them in love, on an individual basis. Male team members should watch out for their female teammates, in case one of the homeless male guests becomes aggressive. If the facility offers showers, team members should point guests toward the showers, prior or after the worship service.

Clean-Up Crew

Some team members may have to be assigned to begin the clean-up effort of the facility.

Order And Decency

Please be also aware that many facilities must adhere to state and federal compliance regarding certain topics they consider politically correct or incorrect. For instance, some facilities may not allow you to talk about same-sex relationships, other religions, or race issues. Therefore, remember to do all things with order and decency, to ensure you will be invited back.

Chapter 9

Permits,

Insurance & Supplies

To conduct a meeting for the homeless, or any other profile of lost souls, in a park or public ground, will require permits from the city in question. Applications must be filed and can be obtained at your local city hall. Call the targeted city hall and explain over the telephone the purpose of your park function, and they will send you the appropriate application and instructions. Fees may be involved depending on the city to file the application.

Each church is required by law to have its own insurance policy, but outreach ministries must also have in place an insurance policy that covers outside events. Ask your church if they will cover such events for you, under their policy. This applies only to events performed on public property, such as parks, parking lots, and other public locations; but do not pertain to events held within the church or a shelter facility.

Remember

Order And Decency

Wherever the Lord may take you as you minister to the homeless and incarcerated, do all things with order and decency, to ensure you will be invited back.

Dedication

Special thanks to Elder D. R. Jones, my family and friends, who prayed and labored with me, while God was birthing this manual.

This manual is dedicated to the 1,600 SOULS that *Just Jesus Ministry* has led to Christ, in the past twelve years, by applying the basic steps outlined in this manual.

And to my precious loved ones, who have gone on into Eternity: my parents, Leon and Dolores Jackson; my life was molded and shaped through their care.

Special thanks also to Joseph Jolivette, my biological father; and to Bobby, my favored and only son, who made my life worth living, by giving me three precious grandchildren: Nicholas, Destani, and Ianna. Loving them has brought great joy and fulfillment to my life.

And special thanks also to my sisters, brothers, nieces and nephews, for their belief in this vision.

Additional Thanks To:

Alice Thomas
The Thomas Family
George and Ramona Morris
Carol Franklin
Minister Patricia Wyatt
Nathan and Elnora Rocha
Pastor Nalinee D. Tillman
Pastor Leemann and Ora Smith.
Dr Vicki M. Lee
Pastor K. S. Bailey
Evangelist. Paulette Johnson
Angelica Marquez
Joyce Gassett
Gayle Thompson
Minister Karen Ashley

And always keeping her memory alive:

Evangelist Renee Moore-English

In My Garden of Gethsemane Prayer

By Chaplain Sharlotte Druex

Father in heaven, I come to you in the name of Jesus.
I pray for the spirit of wisdom, and revelation of knowledge.
Father, give me the fruits of righteousness with discernment in
the name of Jesus. Let the mind of Christ be in me.

Teach me your word with boldness; help me to hold fast to your
word that I may rejoice in the day of Christ. In the name of Jesus
name let me not run in vain.

Renew my mind; create a right spirit in me to forgive. Forgetting
the things behind and reaching forward to those things which are
ahead, cause me to be mature.

Father remove any cup that is not your will and let your will be
done in my life. Order my steps and cause me to not lean on my
own understanding but to acknowledge you in all my ways,
working out my own salvation with fear and trembling. Cause me
to be like a tree planted by the rivers of water; cause all works of
iniquity to depart from me.

Clean me from my secret faults, keep me from presumptuous
sins. Let them have no dominion over me. Father, save your
anointed one. Answer me from your holy heaven.

Redeem me Father from all my troubles, in the name of Jesus.
Lord, I know you will take care of me;

I know you will never leave me or forsake me, and that you are a rewarder to those who diligently seek you. You are the supplier of all my needs.

I give thanks to your holy name. Cause me to be encouraged, so my heart will be strengthened. Cause your angels to encamp around me so that I will be delivered from my weaknesses and addictions.

Cause my steps to be ordered by you and let me not be ashamed in these evil times. Teach me how to wait on you; teach me how to exult you, so that I may inherit my land. Create in me a clean heart, and renew a steadfast spirit in me.

Make your face to shine upon me. Your hands have made me and fashioned me. Teach me your word and your statutes. In the name of Jesus, my children will be delivered and my family will be saved. Teach me how to seek good, so that I will find favor from you and man.

Cause me to have a calm spirit. My heart is in your hand; turn it whatever way you wish. Keep me in perfect peace and keep my mind stayed on you. Lord, you who test the heart will not put more on me than I can bear. Cause my prayers to not be hindered. Bind Satan from taking advantage of me. Write your words on my heart and remove the veil from my heart. Open my eyes to understanding.

Cause me to be humble and not puffed up. Reveal more of your Son to me. Cause me to be holy and without blame. Teach me to walk worthy of the call on my life and let no corrupt communication come from my mouth. Let me not be deceived with empty words. Teach me to put on your whole armor. Teach me to open my mouth with boldness when I speak, so that I may teach your mysteries. Complete your good work in me until Jesus comes. Teach me to run this race to get the prize in Christ Jesus. Teach me to not be anxious for anything and to put on the new man daily. Place in me the fruit of the spirit.

Cause me to stand perfect and complete in your will for me. Help me to not neglect the gifts you have given to me so that I will progress forward. Give me the gift of faith in the name of Jesus. Father as I draw near to you, draw near to me. The prayers of the righteous have much power and I know your ears are open to me. Help me to not want the things of the world.

Teach me to be salt and light to your people. Give me a forgiving heart. Teach me to build my life and your ministry on your solid rock. Open doors that no man can shut, and close doors that no man can open.

Father, keep me from the hour of trials that is coming on the whole world. Father, give me a church after your own heart, and a Pastor to watch out over my soul.

In The Name of Jesus!!

Amen

Thank you for joining Chaplain Sharlotte Druex on her epic journey through tragedy, victory, and anointed ministry.

To correspond with Chaplain Druex, schedule a speaking engagement, and order more copies of this manual, please email:

JustJesus2@gmail.com

Made in the USA
Charleston, SC
26 May 2013

The
Matthew 25
Project

The go-to manual
On ministering to
The homeless and
Incarcerated

Chaplain
Sharlotte Druex

The Matthew 25 Project
Copyright © 2011 by Chaplain Sharlotte Druex

ISBN-13: 978-1469967134
ISBN-10: 1469967138

SOV Books
Norwalk, California
Twww.saintsofvalue.org
A division of Vienna Schilling Books
Fair Oaks, California
www.viennaschilling.us

Printed in the United States of America